Sacajawea's Song

Judith Martin Fuller

Cover and interior design by Sable Books
Illustrations by Mickey Merrell

ISBN 978-0-9913564-9-2

Sable Books
sablebooks.org

Acknowledgements

To the writers who edited the progression and encouraged the publication of *Sacajawea's Song:* Margo Williams, Lucia Robinson, Susan Glave, Nadine York, Dianne Anderson, Lucy Stamm, Brandy Wilson, Janet Ward, Mona Blondis, Susan Boehner, Jack Harlan, Diane Roberts, Mary Bass, Patricia Coe, Joan Kaiser, and Holli Terrell-Cavalluzzi.

*To Sean Fuller and Lauren Justine Fuller,
and to strong women everywhere*

Sacajawea's Song

I Am Sacajawea
November 4, 1804

Toussaint
tells me we leave
on a long trip
with men in white faces

I do not know

I have sixteen years
gather roots and herbs
as the women showed me
live Mandan ways
my world knows these things

a baby grows in me

how can I do this thing
he tells me to do.

The Birth of Jean Baptiste
February 11, 1805

I push and push
I am in great hurt
my baby will not come

Jessaume
smashes two rattlesnake rings
to make sand
he drops them in water
for me to drink

the snake bites my insides
a body slides out
to Captain Lewis

Toussaint calls my baby Jean Baptiste
Clark wraps him in buffalo hide
places him on my breast where
my milk bubbles in great joy

my throat makes happy sounds.

A Thawing Season
Missouri River
April 1, 1805

My heart changes
with each new light

I watch ice break,
swim away,
I watch York pack boats with meat
with many tools I do not know

my heart changes
I am glad Toussaint said
no we will not
go with these men who will
make him work too hard,
stand in the cold

we live outside the Fort

Toussaint waits for the Captains
to not make mad faces,
to break the river's ice

then his heart turns soft,
changes like the river's run,
he says we will leave
with this tribe of white men

he will bring Otter Woman
his other wife

I watch strong backs
pack boats that become
heavy as my heart.

No They Say

My man asks Captains Long Knife and Red Hair
to also take his second wife, Otter Woman,
but they say, "She is big with child, her
bearing on the trail will slow us down,
hinder our going west,
take up boat room, extra food."

"No," they say

my man looks at Otter Woman, says she is no white
woman—she will stop in the morning
catch up by night
the child with her
she is a good woman
will not slow our going, not burden us

"No," they say

at my back, I hear Otter Woman, my almost sister,
captured with me from our home,
grew up here in a strange land,
became Charbonneau's second woman
hears my cries for my brother, my family,
carries my man's second child
I cry as she cries
she cries all the night

now I know the Captains' words
mean what they say.

The Leaving
April 7, 1805

I wrap my son
in his cradleboard, he
sleeps on my back, I
put my feet in the boat,

I look for Otter Woman

she is not here

31 men watch
Jean Baptiste's warm
breath on my neck

Who Wants To See These Things?
April 9-12, 1805

Captain Clark moves a stick
   in a book, makes black marks
   to show where our boat came

Captain Lewis looks at clouds, rain,
   water, plants, fish, birds,
   makes black marks to tell what is here

who wants to see these lines
made by their careful hands

Bird Woman
May 14, 1805

I hear loud shots then two
big black birds squawk
make air swoosh
beneath their wings

I look down river, see men
puff up like angry clouds,
see fat flesh we call whitebear
puff up, too, like a mad porcupine,

both flash long teeth in anger

whitebear chases men
into wild water then
more shots make him dead

I walk away on silent feet
up river, find calm waters,
my dress comes easily down,
warm mud makes sweet
noises between my toes

a soft water blanket
wraps around my legs, reaches
my place to wash the blood
away, comes up to clean me

I lie down to float the soft
moving bed, feel warm sun
touch the place my baby sucks

under the sky two big black birds
circle a silent wind path
on their way to the sun

8

A Big Storm on the Missouri
May 14, 1805

We are in the boat they call safe,
one more time Toussaint turns
boat side to the wind and our sail
falls like a dead tree in a storm

my husband cries to his God
for help, sits like a child
looking at a biting dog

Cruzette yells to Toussaint,
"I will shoot you,"
Says, "do something"

our big white boat rolls
I lean my body over the side,
pull from the water white men's
big tools   papers   books

I find almost all things

I hear men throw out water,
oars move fast in big waves
I see Captains jump up and down,
make loud noises on shore,
see my husband shrink like a snail,
our heavy boat ready to sink

then we blow back to land

I still hold Jean Baptiste
in arms that shake
like loose leaves in wind.

10

Bloodletting
near Maria's River
June 10, 1805

I am so dry my skin
sits on my bones, they
have taken my blood
one time then one more
time to cure me, my skin
longs for blood and water

I am so hot, my skin
hurts, they take me
to the canoe, put me
under a tent
Jean Baptiste sucks
at a dry hot place

I am so thirsty

I am so thirsty

my blood is gone
my milk dries
I hurt in all places

I am dry
as summer sand.

The Withering
June 13, 1805

I hear loud noise
like thunder, hear water
fall, make mist like rain

my eyes will not open
in my head stands my
Shoshoni mother, my brother
Cameahwait, my brown sisters

men give me salts, I sleep
to water sounds crashing down.

I Am Near Death
June 15, 1805

A porcupine sits on my head
sticks, sticks, sticks needles in me
my husband speaks thunder in
my ear, wants me to turn back

needles will go with me, air come out
of my body, I cannot move.

Medicine Man
June 16-21, 1805

My arms jump like hopping frogs
the white medicine man Lewis
drops hot ground water on my tongue,
rubs my skin with bark and opium

my arms stop jumping

he speaks to Labiche
in white man's words
Labiche says French words
to Toussaint who waits all day
to give me Hidatsa words
that say to eat soft foods

I already ate loud foods, raw white
apples, dried fish that
roll inside me, make
the needles come back

Captain Lewis makes fire eyes
at Toussaint, starts once more
with his white medicine

again I am free from hurt

medicine man
gives me quiet, buffalo
soup makes my milk flow.

Flash Flood
June 29, 1805

Jean Baptiste feeds
happy at my breast

I look down
a yellow butterfly
rests on a white bush
her wings pass up and down

the air is quiet

when I look up, it is like night
a roar comes out of sky's mouth
another roar jumps from the ground
noise pushes on my ears
brown water comes rolling fast

I cry out
hold my baby
tight to my breast

a strong wind
beats me down

Charbonneau runs up the hill
reaches for my begging hand

when I touch him
he stands like a big rock
his face does not move

Captain Clark pushes
me from below then we are
above the angry water
that rolls brown circles over
and over Clark's gun, a tomahawk,
an umbrella, a compass
my baby's clothes

and one yellow wing
to calm my fear

Near My People
July 13, 1805

Will they know my face

my heart carries jumping rabbits

we are near my people, they
leave their campfires smoky,
horse tracks deep in the mud,
willow branch houses, bark peeled
for food, the smell of herbs,
story words of my fathers

Shoshoni carry my blood
sign my baby's skin and eyes
I wish to touch their brown faces
sniff the smoked hides
that wrap my elders' dried up shoulders
watch soft eyes that look
like hawks at my strange new tribe.

York
July 22, 1805

Sun pours hot on York's skin
blacker and blacker his heavy
load, he does not see me watch
his sad eyes that worried for me
when the flood waters broke

he makes ready the ground for
my bed, Indian walks sacred
soil, his voice quiet as mine, his
skin different as mine and I want
to know if his babies sleep well,
if his arms ache for my Jean Baptiste.

A Mouse in the Eagle's Claw
July 30, 1805

Then I was like a mouse
behind a tree with my brother
when powerful Hidatsas came like
thunder into our camp, my eyes
opened with fear, my tongue dry
I could not fight those claws
that found me, tore me from my tribe

the captains think I
do not remember
think I only want food
my baby   beads   baskets

I do remember

my bones shake here at
three rivers, again I become
a mouse in the eagle's claw
my hands wet like skin
of Shoshoni salmon.

Beaver's Head
August 8, 1805

I see

I see

I see

big rocks growing
out from valley floor
I know them

I tell Captain Lewis we near
agaidekas Shoshoni who eat salmon
tukudeka Shoshoni who eat sheep
my brother Cameahwait

these people have horses
guides for us

Lewis moves fast toward the rocks
that look like beaver's teeth
knows my word is true.

Shame
August 14, 1805

Charbonneau's huge hand rises
hits hard my face
my throat closes, my food
will not go down, there is
fog around my ears

Captain Clark's body goes
stiff like an angry wolf
he stands above my husband
who does not look up
the captain's eyes flash red
he roars to Charbonneau to stop

again I become a dog
to my husband, I hide
in my tent, my cheeks hot
like fire that burns in my heart.

Skins

I wake, crawl quietly past Toussaint,
his hand twitches, stops me now
for a moment before I rise, walk away
into mountain night air toward the Captains

Captain Clark hears, raises his head, throws off
deerskins that cover him,
walks toward me

"You're shaking, squar," he says to me,
"You need more skins to stop your legs
from looking weak."

he covers me in skins, touches
my shoulder, wraps me
in his blanket

for a moment my head rests against him
a peaceful pounding of his heart calms
my shaking arms
he looks down to me

"I cannot let his hands hurt you," he says
"He acts bad to you like the snake
that waits under the rock to strike.
I cannot let him strike you like that snake."

I look at the ground, wait for red
to leave my face.

"Toussaint is my husband," I say,
" the father of Jean Baptiste,
the man who brings me to you.
I do not hate him for that."

from his place on the grass, Toussaint rises,
moves his head this way and that in the dark,
smells for my presence
"You leave me here," he says,
"alone in the dark, squaw girl."

my feet do not think
I move closer to the Captain
I speak to Toussaint in Hidatsu.
"I am here."

my eyes down, I give the Captain his skins,
open my skin to the cold
of Toussaint's bed.

Shallow Water
August 16, 1805

Low in the river's water I sit
quietly in Captain Clark's canoe
know he takes me home, I
am silent as the rattlesnake
who waits for us on shore
my body hungers to touch
this man who protects me.

Coming Home
August 17, 1805

Toward blue sky I see two bodies
both wear my people's clothes
my heart beats my chest
our canoe comes closer, closer

then I step on Shoshoni ground
suck my fingers to say this is my tribe
my head sings with tree birds

here stands my old friend who
ran from Hidatsa when I
could not run, I cannot stop
the birds happy sound
her hug pushes out the song.

Two Bodies
August 17, 1805

The Captains call me, I
go inside the Chief's tent
smell meats and roots cook
become a small girl again
sit with my head down

Captains tell me promises
to make of guns and gifts
from somewhere far away
my words go to Chief's ears
he listens
to my Shoshoni voice

when I look up
I see Chief's brown eyes

I know his eyes

my arms shake, eyes make water
I cannot sit so quiet, my legs
push my body up, I scream to
Chief Cameahwait, my brother my brother

he looks at me, sees his
Shoshoni sister, I cannot stop, I throw
my small blanket on his big shoulders
he sees my eyes water, talks very fast

his words run a spear to my heart
my family is dead he says

I become two bodies now
one with joy
one with sorrow.

First Hunger
August 22, 1805

Cameahwait's stomach goes in like
a bear's cave, I can see his bones
I give him small sugars, he eats
my captains' squash

he says these are the best things
he has ever eaten.

A Snake Around My Heart
August 25, 1805

I know this is true

soon Shoshoni secretly leave for
buffalo hunting grounds
my brother tells them
go like summer birds

I know this is true

my Captains do not understand
Shoshoni way, think the next
sun will see Indian tents, Indian
horses to carry their heavy loads

my mouth does not know
on which side to speak

quietly I tell Charbonneau
of my brother's plan

I know I have chosen

around my heart
my words release a snake.

In the Bitterroots
September 11, 1805

Men eat clean the bones
of wolves   dogs   horses

it is not enough

we make our death march
through these stony mountain paths

my milk comes slow, again Jean
Baptiste cries at a dry spot
a bare land where milk should run

I carry him close, hum
my soft songs to forget
his sinking eyes and cheeks.

War Feathers
October 15, 1805

We near Nez Perce

war feathers flap
make bright red anger
below blue cloudless sky

I show my brown face
Jean Baptiste on my hip
walk quiet steps forward

their feathers come down
leave calm air.

32

Janey's Vote
November 24, 1805

What is this vote they say I have to winter
here or there, a choice to do this or that

I want the choice to find wild licorice root,
white apple root, for others to find
great waters

my vote is to stay near
food, to bed my baby down
they call me Janey to make my vote count,
the place where we camp Fort Clatsop

I peel my rotted leather
skin from my back

winter in.

Gifts
December 25, 1805

I.

Captain Clark's bones wore only skin
his hands dried up to little bird's feet

from flour hidden for Jean Baptiste
I made bread to feed Clark's longing

II.

Indians wanted blue chief beads
raindrops that sparkled like
water in sunlight
I gave my blue bead belt
they gave me blue sealskin coat

III.

today the day of white men's
gifts I dig deep down, find
my twenty-four weasel tails
as beautiful as seal skin
or blue raindrop beads
or loaves of bread

I lay them in my Captain's hands
he rubs the tails over and over
and from his own river a drop
falls on all that I have.

On Seeing the Whale
January 6, 1806

They say there sleeps the biggest fish

I do not know if this is true

I saw a bigger fish in the
Bitterroots deep in Jean Baptiste's
eyes that screamed for mother's milk
for warmth in women's arms

in Toussaint his heavy love
on my tired body his weakness
full as these waters

I saw a bigger fish
on York's shoulders with
weight so heavy he bends
to meet the ground

I do not open wide my eyes
to this big fish
that awes these men.

Look At Me

My son!
Look at me!

I remembered what women taught me

I gathered seeds to dry
dug ground with my stick
found roots that mice buried
under the wood

I helped keep these men alive

I was strong for you
my son

look at me.

What Will I Do
The Return

Here near the river of hot waters
Captain Clark gives a name to big rocks
he calls them Pompey's Tower and
kisses my baby by the rushing waters
he calls Baptiste's Creek

we are near home and eat roots
I dug high in Nez Perce country
what will I do

he calls me the squar
I watched him touch the sick ones,
watched him close a wound
when the man with one
eye shot his friend

my husband took my two dresses
to give the Nez Perce for horses

I will be home soon
what will I do

my Captains promise great things
to the Indians and I tell them in their
words they will have beads and food,
tell them the men who send us
promise great peace and no war

Jean Baptiste burned in his skin
and I pressed him close, he will
be home soon

what will I do

here is the place I understand
mosquitoes cover my eyes like
a blanket of darkness, my head
drawn down

 I do not know
what I will do.